W9-CSU-887

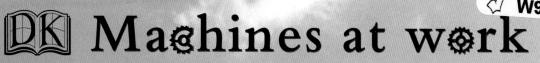

Machines at work

DIGGER

DK

LONDON, NEW YORK, MUNICH,
MELBOURNE, and DELHI

Written and edited by Nicola Deschamps
Designed by Susan Calver
Additional design Helen Chapman,
Jacqueline Gooden, and Cheryl Telfer

Publishing Manager Susan Leonard
Managing art editor Clare Shedden
Jacket design Bob Warner
Picture researcher Sarah Stewart-Richardson
Production Janet Levesley
DTP Designer Almudena Díaz
Consultant J. Bowles

First American Edition, 2004

Published in the United States by
DK Publishing, Inc.
375 Hudson Street
New York, New York 10014

06 07 10 9 8 7 6 5 4 3 2 1

Copyright © 2004 Dorling Kindersley Limited
First paperback edition 2006

All rights reserved under International and Pan-American Copyright Conventions. No part
of this publication may be reproduced, stored
in a retrieval system, or transmitted in any form or by any means, electronic, mechanical,
photocopying, recording or otherwise,
without the prior written permission of the copyright owner.
Published in Great Britain by Dorling Kindersley Limited.

Library of Congress Cataloging-in-Publication Data

Deschamps, Nicola
  Digger / by Nicola Deschamps.-- 1st American ed.
    p. cm. -- (Machines at work)
Summary: Illustrations and simple text describe machines that are used
in road and house building, forestry, and mining industries.
  ISBN-13 978-0-7566-0216-1 ISBN-10 0-7566-0216-5 (hardcover)
  ISBN-13 978-0-7566-1907-7 ISBN-10 0-7566-1907-6 (pbk.)
  1. Excavating machinery--Juvenile literature. [1. Machinery.] I.
Title. II. Machines at work (DK Publishing, Inc.)
TA732 .D47 2004
629.225--dc22
                                        2003018503

Color reproduction by Media Development and Printing Ltd., UK
Printed and bound in China by Toppan Printing Co., Ltd.

Discover more at

www.dk.com

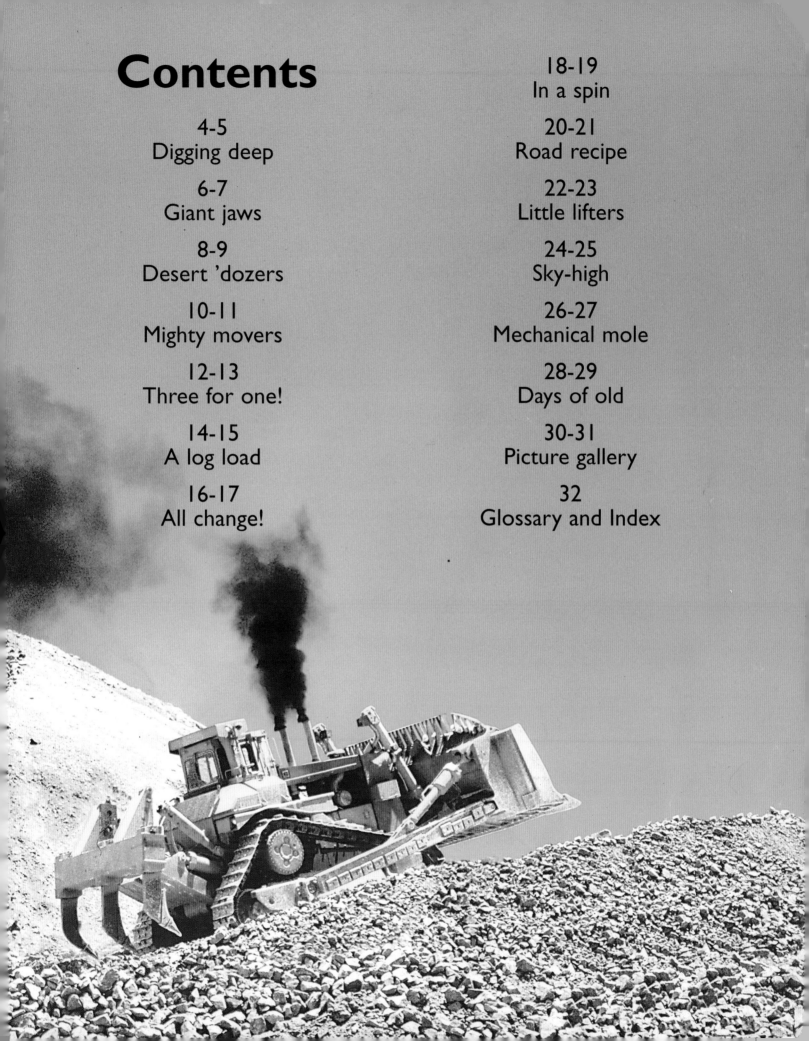

Contents

Digging deep

Excavators come in all shapes and sizes, and there are some that run on **tracks**, while others have **wheels**.

This excavator can run over uneven ground easily and safely on these wide crawler tracks.

VOLVO

Creeping crawlers
A crawler track is made up of lots of separate pieces that fit together to form a flexible band, which is driven by sprockets or wheels.

This big excavator can dig and lift over 14 tons (13 metric tons) of rubble. That's as heavy as three elephants!

Big bucket

This excavator is using a bucket attachment that has sharp teeth. These help it to cut through soil and rubble.

Stick

Boom

Wheelies

This little wheeled excavator can run almost as fast as a car, so it can be easily transported from one site to another. The boom and stick can be safely folded away while on the road.

It's a fact

🦾 The Komatsu PCO1 is a tiny excavator; it's the size of a motorcycle!

🦾 A giant mining excavator is so big that the operator has to climb up a stepladder to reach the cab!

Giant jaws

This mighty machine works in the **demolition** industry and can rip apart a house in just two hours! It bites into buildings, demolishing them bit by bit.

This muncher attachment can tear down steel structures and crush concrete floors.

Crunch!

Munch!

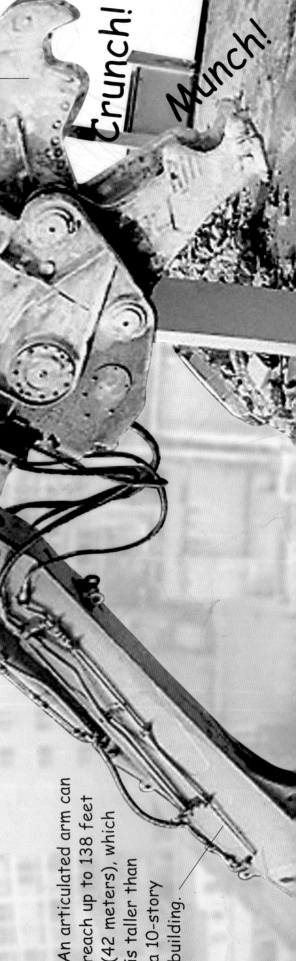

Boom!

Explosives are used mostly to demolish high-rise buildings—a 20-story building can be destroyed in just four seconds!

An articulated arm can reach up to 138 feet (42 meters), which is taller than a 10-story building.

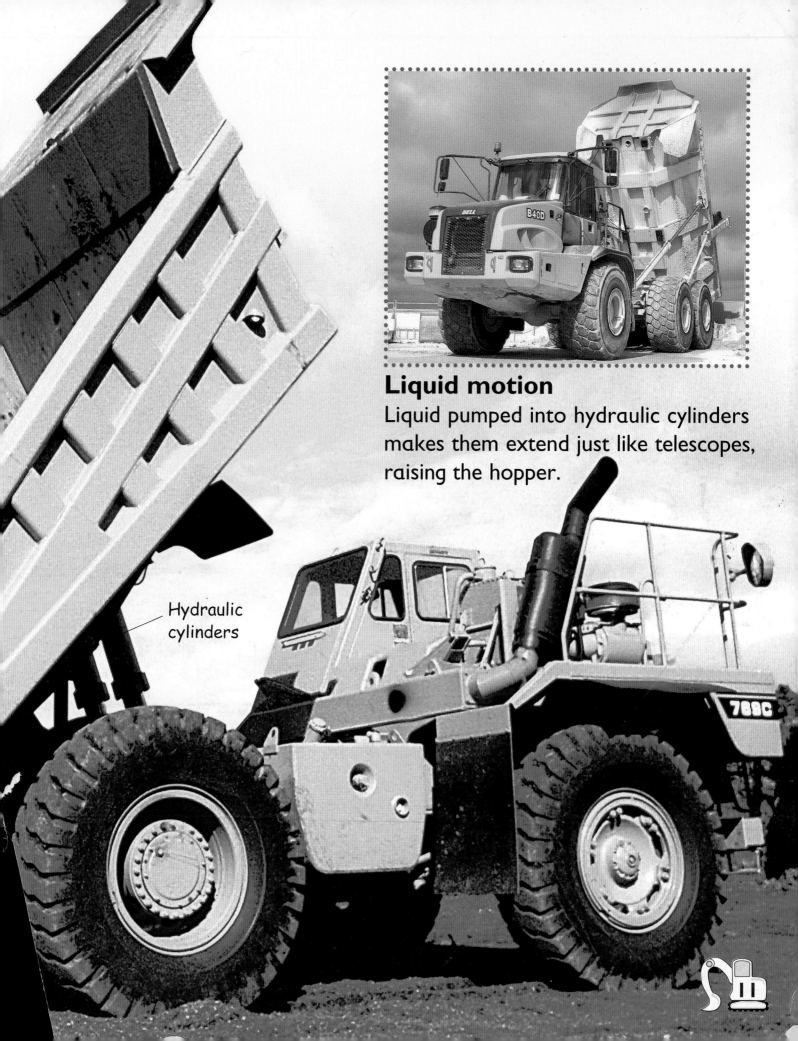

Liquid motion

Liquid pumped into hydraulic cylinders makes them extend just like telescopes, raising the hopper.

Hydraulic cylinders

Three for one!

A backhoe loader is a **tractor**, **loader**, and **backhoe** rolled into one. It's small, versatile, quick on its wheels, and very strong.

Boom

Stick

Bucket

Loader
The loader acts like a big scoop. It is used to pick up and carry materials such as soil, rocks, and stones.

BL71

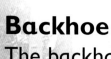

Backhoe

The backhoe is the main tool and is used for digging and lifting heavy loads. It comes in three parts: boom, stick, and bucket.

It's a fact

The driver can turn his seat to face the front or the back of the machine.

The backhoe has a greater range of movement than the loader as it has connecting joints, just like your arm!

Stabilizer legs stop this machine from bouncing around or tipping over while digging.

Loader   Tractor   Backhoe

Tractor

Just like a farm tractor, this backhoe loader has a powerful engine, big, tough tyres, and a cab with steering controls.

A log load

This powerful wheel loader is carrying whole **tree trunks** inside its log-grab attachment. It will carry this heavy load to a nearby sawmill.

Scoop, carry, dump
Wheel loaders are used to pick up earth, rocks, and rubble. They then empty their load into the back of a dump truck, which carries it away.

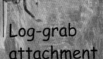
Log-grab attachment

Snap!

Break it up

This excavator is equipped with a breaker. By using this attachment, the operator can drill lots of big holes into a concrete floor. The more holes drilled, the quicker the concrete will crack and break into pieces.

In a spin

The enormous **drum** on this concrete mixer turns constantly to prevent the wet **concrete** inside from setting and becoming unusable.

Chute

Made by hand
Small cement mixers do much the same job as the large industrial concrete mixers. However, it's a worker who loads the raw materials into the drum, and not machines.

Drum

Firm foundations

By using a vibrator, this worker can break up the thick, sticky concrete that has been poured in, allowing it to flow more easily into the gaps.

Mixed delivery

The drum turns one way to mix the concrete, and the other way to empty it out. The wet concrete comes out of the drum and pours down the chute.

It's a fact

Wet concrete is acidic and can burn if it stays in contact with your skin.

The driver can operate the drum by remote control.

Concrete is a mixture of sand, small stones, cement, and water.

Road recipe

Making a **road** is noisy, dusty, hot, and steamy. Machines must dig, carry, scrape, push, and spread before a road is ready for you to **drive** on!

Blade

Smooth operator
Before a road can be laid, the ground must be made smooth. The top, bumpy layer is scraped off by this grader's metal blade.

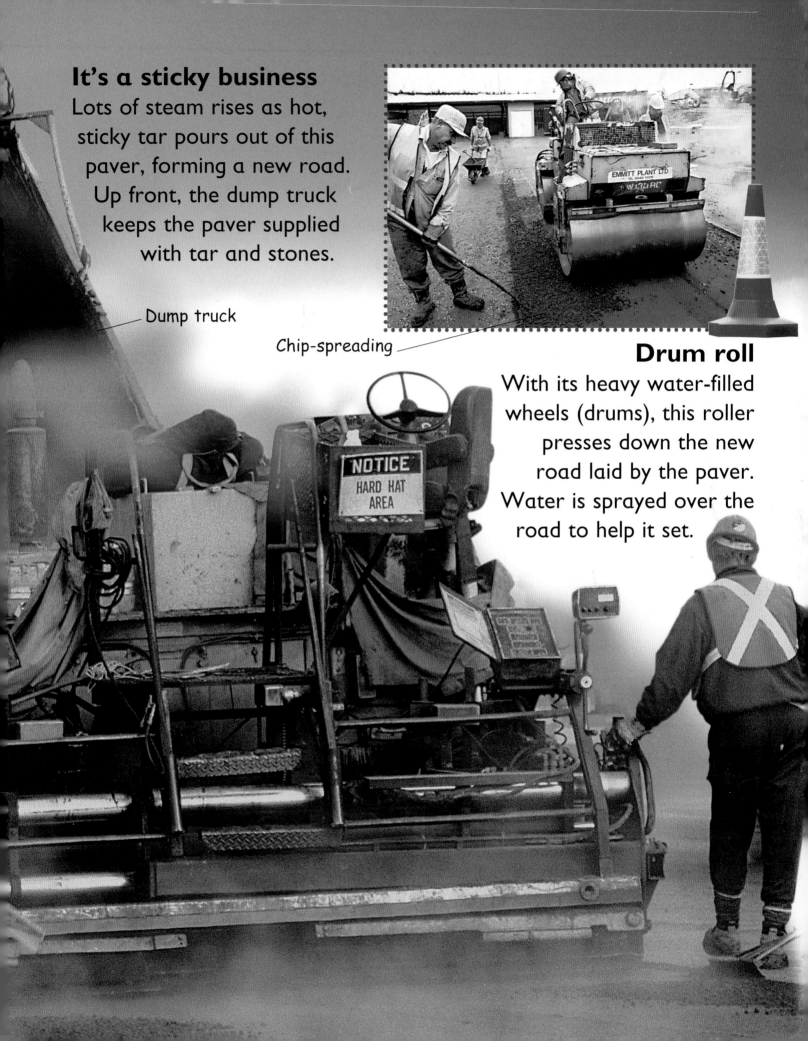

It's a sticky business

Lots of steam rises as hot, sticky tar pours out of this paver, forming a new road. Up front, the dump truck keeps the paver supplied with tar and stones.

Dump truck

Chip-spreading

Drum roll

With its heavy water-filled wheels (drums), this roller presses down the new road laid by the paver. Water is sprayed over the road to help it set.

NOTICE
HARD HAT
AREA

EMMITT PLANT LTD
W130 AC

Little lifters

These machines are an ideal size to zip in and out of **narrow** spaces, carrying loads in a warehouse, busy city, or on a building site.

Keep it clean
A diesel-run engine can produce soot that would dirty these paper rolls. Therefore, this forklift is powered by gas.

Gas cylinder

Spinning wheel
The wheels on a skid steer can spin in opposite directions allowing the driver to turn around in the smallest possible area.

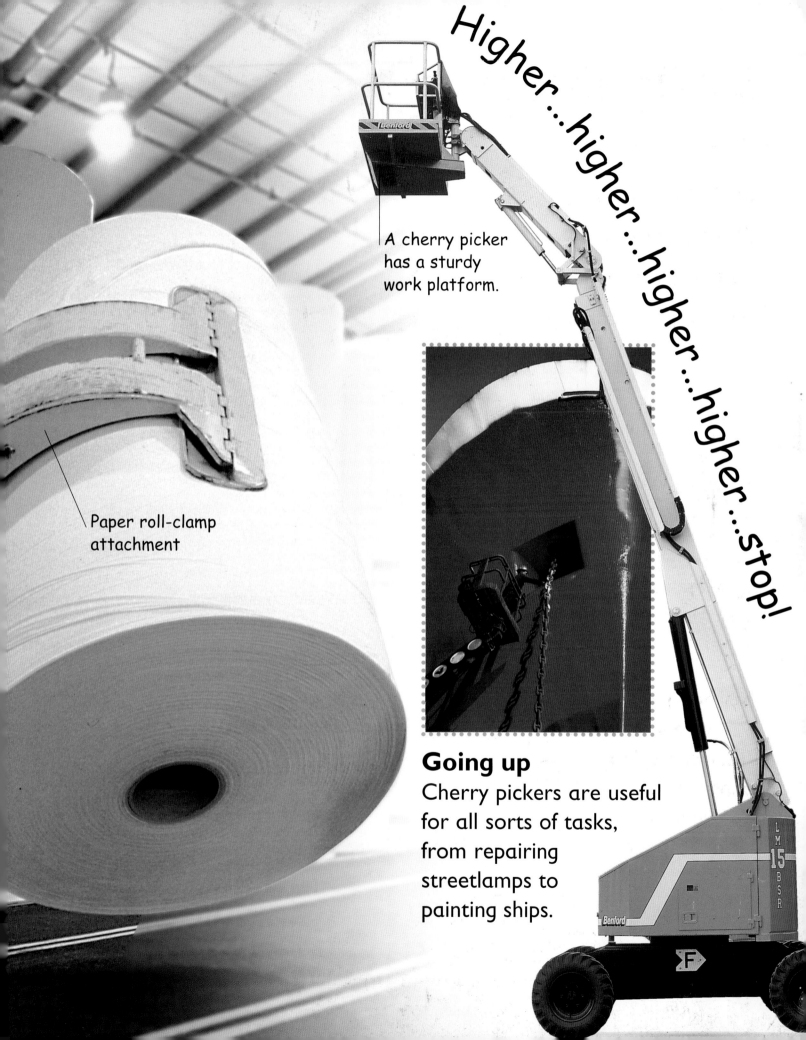

Higher...higher...higher...higher...stop!

A cherry picker has a sturdy work platform.

Paper roll-clamp attachment

Going up

Cherry pickers are useful for all sorts of tasks, from repairing streetlamps to painting ships.

Sky-high

Cranes are the tallest machines in the world. They reach high into the sky and can lift massive loads, from huge metal beams to whole boats!

On the move
Installed on a special truck, this mobile crane can be driven from site to site. Its arm extends like a telescope.

Jib

This is a small gas-production platform.

Floating cranes
Off-shore drilling stations are built with the help of special cranes that are placed on a huge boat (barge).

Operator's cab

Bird's-eye view

From a small cab far above the city skyline, the operator can control the arm movements of this towering crane.

Tower

Crane barge

Mechanical mole

With its huge spinning **head** and razor-sharp **teeth**, this massive tunnel-boring machine can **cut** through earth, under a seabed, or even through a mountain!

Cutting head

It's a fact

This amazing machine cleans up after itself, removing rubble with an internal conveyor belt. All that is left behind is a smooth, clean tunnel, ready for development.

TML 430 T

It's a heavyweight
A powerful crane is needed to lift this boring machine into place, since it weighs more than 300 cars!

Rocky road

Fitted with 48 tough cutter discs, this huge cutter head can slice through solid rock.

This machine is longer than a football field!

whirr....whirr....whirr....whirr....whirr

Sea trains

Far below the sea, this tunnel-boring machine is busy digging beneath the seabed, making tunnels that will be used by trains.

Days of old

Some of the amazing **machines** you see today weren't around years ago—**people** did the work instead!

Many hands make light work

Teamwork was important, and everyone had specific jobs to do. It took a lot of people-power to make just one building—look at all these workers!

It's a fact

🐾 Using a broom attachment, a skid steer can sweep up to 10 times faster than you could!

🐾 A big bulldozer could shovel more dirt in just a few seconds than you could in a whole week!

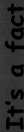

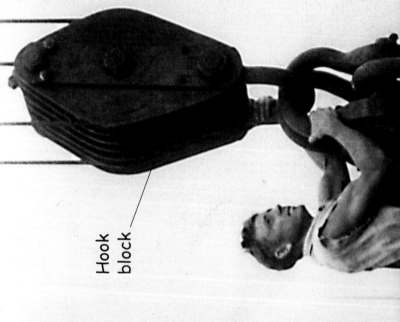

Hook block

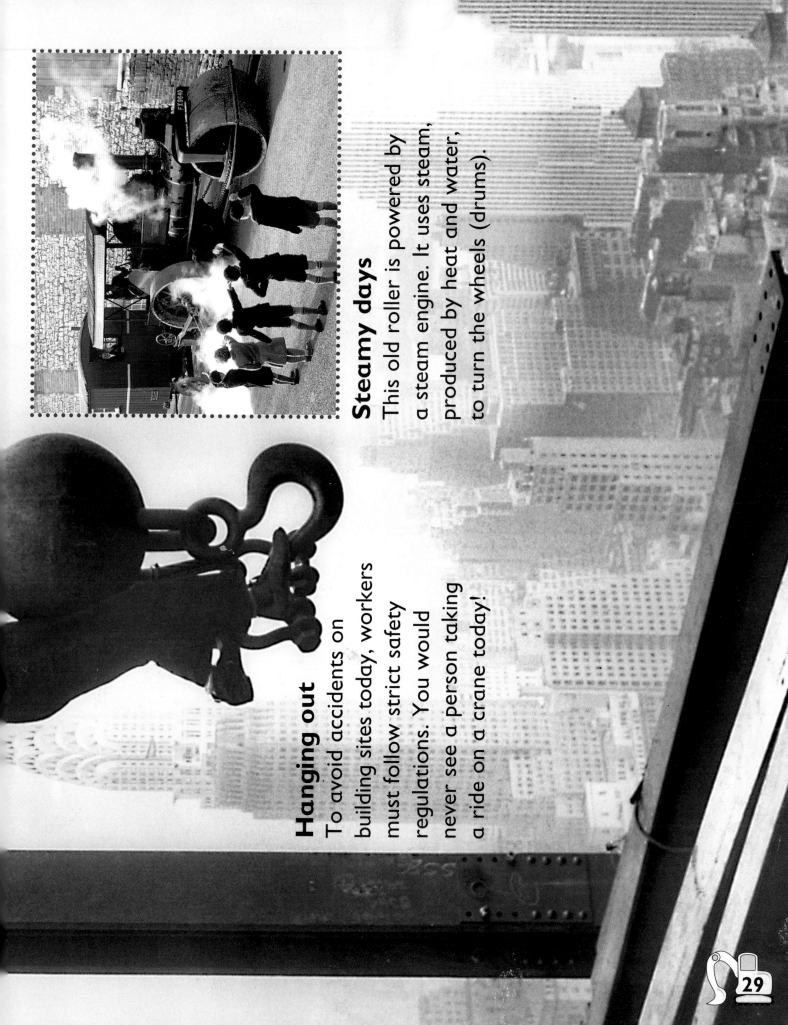

Steamy days

This old roller is powered by a steam engine. It uses steam, produced by heat and water, to turn the wheels (drums).

Hanging out

To avoid accidents on building sites today, workers must follow strict safety regulations. You would never see a person taking a ride on a crane today!

Picture gallery

Wheel loader

Some wheel loaders have metal wheel covers that protect the wheels from sharp rocks and stones.

Forklift

Just like the big machines, forklifts must use flashing hazard lights to warn people that they are nearby.

Roller

There are plugs on each roller drum that allow water to be added or removed.

Crane

A computer works out how much a crane can lift at different points along its arm (jib).

Concrete mixer

A mixer's drum must be cleaned out after use to avoid a buildup of hard concrete.

Backhoe loader

The backhoe loader is the most useful machine on a small building site, since it has tools at the front and back.

Excavator

An excavator can dig on one side and dump on the other because its top half spins all the way around.

Attachments

Some machines have more than 13 different kinds of attachments that they can use.

Dump truck

Giant dump trucks are moved from site to site in pieces because they are too big to travel on roads.

Bulldozer

If a machine gets stuck in the mud, a bulldozer can be used to help dig it out or push it clear.

Glossary

Articulated arm has two or more parts connected by joints.

Boom the back part of a machine's arm.

Bucket the scoop of a digging machine.

Counterbalance a static weight that balances a lifted weight.

Chute a channel that directs loose material.

Drum a hollow, barrel-shaped container filled with liquid, such as water.

Demolition the controlled destruction of buildings.

Diesel a fuel used to power engines.

Explosive a material that blows up when lit by an electrical current.

Hydraulic the movement of machine parts that is powered by a liquid, such as oil.

Hopper a container for carrying heavy loads.

Load the material carried by machines.

Engine a machine that burns fuel to make a vehicle work.

Jib the horizontal part of a machine's arm.

Stabilizers the steel legs that stop a stationary vehicle from tipping over.

Stick the first part of a machine's arm just behind the attachment.

Tar a thick, black material used for road-building.

Mining excavator

Acknowledgements

Dorling Kindersley would like to thank Squibb and Davies (Demolition) Ltd, Volvo Construction Equipment Ltd, CNH France, Controlled Demolition Ltd, Komatsu UK, National Maritime Museum, London, Finning (UK) Ltd Caterpillar, and Barloworld Handling Ltd.

Index

Picture credits:

The publisher would like to thank the following for their kind permission to reproduce their photographs: t=top, b=bottom, r=right, l=left, c=center

1 Volvo Construction Equipment Ltd.; **2-3** Corbis: Lester Lefkowitz; **4-5** Volvo Construction Equipment Ltd., **4bl** Corbis: Charles O'Rear, **5tr** Komatsu; **6-7** Conrad Blakemore: Squibb & Davies Demolition Ltd, **6l** Corbis: Graig Hammell, **7tr** Corbis: Roger Ressmeyer; **8-9** Corbis: Christine Osborne, **9t** Corbis: Ralph White, **9r** Corbis: Carl & Ann Purcell; **10-11&31bl** Corbis: Paul Steele, **10l** Corbis: Andy Hibbert; Ecoscene **11tr** Alvey and Towers; **12-13** Volvo Construction Equipment Ltd.,**12l** Caterpillar Inc., **13br** JCB; **14-15** Corbis: Charles Mauzy, **14-15b** Corbis: Lester Lefkowitz, **14l&15tr** Construction Photography.com: Jean-Francois Cardella; **16-17&31tr** Corbis: Raymond Gehman, **16bl** Construction Photography.com: Xavier de Canto, **16bc** Corbis: Colin garratt; Milepost 92, **16br** Case New Holland, **17r** Conrad Blakemore: Squibb & Davies Demolition; **18-19** Construction Photography.com: Chris Henderson, **18l** Zefa Picture Library: M. Idem, **19tr** Construction Photography.com: QA Photos/Jim Byrne; **20-21** Masterfile UK: Gloria H. Chomica, **20l** Caterpillar Inc.: Finning (UK) Ltd, **21tr&30bc** Construction Photography.com: David Stewart-Smith; **22-23&30tr** Corbis: Lester Leftkowitz, **22l** John Deere/ Pharo Communications, **23c** Corbis: Vince Streano; **24-25** Alamy Images: Peter Bowater, **24tl** Construction Photography.com: Adrian Greeman, **25tl** Alamy Images: Pictures Colour Library.com, **25tr** Corbis Sygma: Eranian Philippe; **26-27** US Department of Energy, **26tl** Corbis Sygma: Polak Matthew, **26cl** Corbis Sygma: Jacques Langevin, **27b** © QA Photos Ltd.: Jim Byrne; **28-29** Corbis: Bettmann, **28tl** Royalty Free Images: Getty Images, **29tl** Alamy Images: Popperfoto; **30-31** Getty Images: Per Eriksson, **30bl** Construction Photography.com: David Stewart-Smith; **31tc** Case New Holland; **32-33** Corbis: Bob Rowan; Progressive Image.

All other images © Dorling Kindersley
For further information see: www.dkimages.com